Xtreme
sports

Publisher/President — Rick McMillen
Vice President/Chief Financial Officer — Marna McMillen
Vice President/Director of Publishing Operations — Sir McMillen

Executive Editor — Jim Carley
Research Editor — Jim Walden
Research Assistants — Laura Friedman, Jennifer Condi, Amber Mayne

Creative Director — Jeff Wolf
Design/Graphics — David Medina, Cheryl Leary
Design/Graphics/Production — Aaron Brittain
Photography — Tom Sanders, David Major, Aerial Focus; Tom Stillo;
Kelly Kingman; Nick Adams; Bill Alkofer; John Stack; Bud Fawcett; Adventure Photo;
Tom Hauck; Shane Babin; Todd Pointing; Russell Hoover; Sean Manning; Brad Wrobleski;
Gordon Wiltsu; Eric Evans; Jean Pierre Vollrath; Andy Anderson; Jorge Salas; Randy Bloomfield;
Marc Kozai; Vince Cavataio; Geoff Ragatz; A. Scoggins; Jon Mozo; John Schnack; Torey Piro,
Andy Tullis; Cynis Navabpour; Melinda Maxfield; Temple Cummins; Stan Evans; Chris Murray;
Damea Dorsey; Anthony Cappa; James Cassimus; Cody Steele; Kirk Bender;
Mike Simi; Andy Belcher, Wade McKoy; A. Zins
Cover Illustration — Rick McMillen

Circulation Manager — Bambi McMillen
Data Processing — Danette Daniel, Erin Folks, Adrian Jackson,
Kudirat Muhammed, Jessica Ortega, Diane Thorne

Business Manager — Bobbye Jean Smith
Executive Assistant — Stormy Waters

Advertising Director — Al Allen
Corporate Sales Director — Harvey Hooker
Advertising Coordinator — Tiffany McMillen
http://www.mcmillencomm.com

3301 Allen Parkway, Houston, TX 77019
P.O. Box 2608, Houston, TX 77252
http://www.gulfpub.com/books.html

ISBN# 0-88415-909-4
Gulf Publishing Company

Library of Congress Catalog Card Number: 98-073064

The essence of this Xtreme Sports book is not the danger of the individual challenges or the skill of the photographers and artists, though this book would not have been created were it not for those key factors.

The essence is the people who are involved in these baffling, idiosyncratic pursuits. They are special people with unique perspectives on life and death. They are the skiers who crash down impossible inclines, the B.A.S.E. jumpers who leap from dizzying heights and the surfers who cloak themselves in monster waves. No chains can hold them. No pyschologist can explain them. No average person can understand them.

But to each of these athletes who grace the pages of this book, we tip our hat.

Xtreme
contents

Like the negative of a photograph, the personalities of extreme sports participants are night-and-day different from those of the average person. Lurking deep in their psyches is an inner drive precisely opposite of those "normal" people who gravitate toward safety, security, comfort and calm in their everyday lives.

There lies within most of us a mechanism that insists on security, safety and protection to the fullest. We lock our doors, bolt our windows, fasten our seat belts and activate our burglar alarms. All to be sheltered and secure. It's a natural tendency among the masses.

To most humans, for instance, travel on an airplane is merely a mostly bothersome means to an end. Many even fear flying. But to the extreme athlete, an airplane is only the stepping stone to the real trip — leaping into space thousands of feet up and from there, anything goes. Sky surfing, sky diving in formation, you name it. Why would anyone, you have to wonder, want to leave the safety and serenity of a perfectly good airplane?

Of course, that's not even the limit any more for sky-divers. They have gone on to B.A.S.E jumping, that rogues' world of parachuting from anything fixed. Mostly illegal and even more perilous, B.A.S.E jumping takes sky diving to the next illogical conclusion. B.A.S.E. (stands for Buildings, Antennas, Spans — or bridges — and Earth — or cliffs) has only been around for the last 20 years or so as we know it but is fast setting the standard for ultimate thrill-seeking.

It is a measure of the B.A.S.E jumpers' disdain for deliverance that there are 450 recorded members of the B.A.S.E. Association and there are 39 other official members who have died while engaged in their "sport." That's nearly one of every 12 who have died seeking their thrills, pursuing that ultimate high or whatever it is that drives them on to plummet off of surfaces that barely are tall enough to enable them time to get their parachutes deployed.

Not all extreme sports, of course, inherently defy death. But the word extreme lets you know that it is no normal pursuit. Surfing and bodyboarding seemed tame enough back in the 1960s when Annette Funicello and Frankie Avalon were in all those popular beach movies. But much of the surfing done today is off the Northern coasts of Hawaii and California as well as Peru and Mexico, where waves reach the height of small buildings.

And if that wasn't enough thrills, many surfers have graduated to "wakeboarding," which takes the tame element of surfing and revs it up several notches behind a motor boat. The very intent is to hit the wake of the boat over and over, spinning, flipping, jumping and diving, while hanging on to the rope attached to the boat.

Simple water skiing usually involves avoiding the wake. Even stunt water skiing does little more than engage lifts and other skiers. But wakeboarding is a crash a minute, all by yourself.

That then is the essence of extreme sports — taking the normal to the abnormal, the ordinary to the extraordinary. It's not enough, for example, to just roller skate anymore. Now they must be in-line skates, designed to accelerate better and take the curves more evenly.

It's not enough to skateboard. Now they must skateboard on half-pipes and obstacle courses, constructed to maximize the thrill and the danger.

And it's not enough to take a leisurely ride on a bicycle. Now it has to be a mountain bike and the rider and the bike both must challenge the toughest mountains, taking it to the extreme all the way up and down.

Extreme thus has become a state of mind for many people today. And it obviously says something about our society in general. Everywhere you look, the world of the extreme seems to be creeping into our lives.

Action movies today can only be judged by their shock value. Stuntmen and women attempt almost incomprehensible feats as each movie steps farther and farther into the realm of the unbelievable.

Likewise, the once considered exciting, old-time roller-coaster rides are passé. Only the extreme roller coasters of today's wild theme parks, rides that are contrived to leave the riders as discombobulated as possible, will suffice. No thrills, no paying customers seems to be the rule. No harm, no howl.

It is perhaps the legacy of a society that has replaced sipping ice tea on the front porch with drive-by shootings.

Our ultra-fast, often brutal world rarely allows one the luxury of relaxing anywhere or any time. So it's only natural that such a culture would have to go to the extremes in its sports and sports viewing. Like the skier who's no longer satisfied with the advanced slopes — so he or she must dive out of a helicopter onto a near 90-degree precipice. Or the once serene canoeist who now isn't happy anywhere except in a kayak battling nature — and a few big boulders — in white-water rapids. That's the norm for the extreme athlete who seems to proliferate around the world. Once the realm of only a few sensational "daredevils," tens of thousands now participate in these life-threatening pursuits on land, air and water and extreme sports seem now to speak to the very heart of our society. If you haven't competed or dreamed of competing, you have watched in wonder.

That fascination has given birth to this book. It is an attempt to identify if not explain, illustrate if not participate. In words, pictures and paintings, the sprawling exhilaration of white-water kayaking comes roaring into your world as does the adrenaline rush of wing-walking, the mind-blowing terror of B.A.S.E jumping and the vivid intensity of ice-climbing. Wherever humans go to defy death, this book has ventured to record it.

Through the magical cameras of some of the world's best sports photographers, you experience extreme sports at its most extreme. And just as normal pictures demand normal presentation, these extreme photos can only be displayed in profound layouts. Our hope is that you can vicariously jump through the pages with our extreme participants. Step by step, leap by leap through these pages the reader can peer into the domain and perhaps the mindset of the most dangerous endeavors men and women can conceive. This is a smorgasbord of stimulation from as close as you can be without actually risking your life.

Sit back, but don't relax, as you wander through the world of the extreme. And hang onto your chair. There are no seat belts here.

XTREME
Ice-climbing

Dr. Jim Frey

Whenever you turn on ESPN or ESPN2 these days, you won't necessarily find football or basketball or baseball. And often not even golf, volleyball, racing or softball. Nowadays you have just as good a chance of seeing one of the new sports they call "extreme."

To some, extreme sports are for the demented, the individuals who are on the fringe of sanity. But to those who have studied them, extreme athletes aren't as far out on the mental scale as you might expect.

Dr. James H. Frey is a respected sociologist at the University of Nevada Las Vegas who has studied the phenomenon we call "extreme sports athletes." He believes for the most part those athletes are really more normal than anyone would guess.

And he says few of them really have the "death wish" many people believe is imbedded in their psyches.

"They don't see what they are doing as death-defying," Frey says. "There's a concept out there that is very interesting called edgework. They take themselves out to the edge, the boundaries, but they don't go over the edge. Sky-divers as well as most other extreme athletes are pushing the edge but they're not going over it because they think they are controlling it.

"They're in control. They've packed their own chutes, they've gone through

the training. They're with pilots and others who know what to do. So if they do die, it's their fault. Something they did in the preparation. So they see themselves as in control.

As much as they might seem to be renegades, Frey says one might be surprised by the conservative everyday lives extreme athletes often lead.

"These guys are not rounders," Frey says. "They're controlled, motivated, accomplished people and they approach their sports that way. This gives them a challenge, a matter of control and self-determination. And there is some research that says this is kind of a source of excitement not found in other settings that are commonly associated with sports participation. It's never really been proven, but this special kind of excitement may be one of the reasons they engage in these sports."

Frey says you might not even be able to tear an extreme athlete away from his or her sport.

"The other side of the coin is that these people do not have what we call `risk-propense personalities,'" he says. "They're not seeking a thrill in everything they do. We have some research that shows that these people tend not to participate in other risky sports. They don't gamble much.

"Fully 90 percent of the time, they wear their seat belts. They don't invest in speculative stocks. If they invest at all, it might be in government bonds. They may be thrill seekers but they're not stimulus addicts. They like the feelings they get when they do dive or do their snowboarding acrobatics or when the extreme skiers jump from helicopters onto the steepest slopes. But the rest of the time, they like things to be very safe.

"They're still able to control what's happening even though they're on the edge. They're not out of control. These people are not flaming weirdos. Even though you might think, `Who would do something like this? They must be nuts.'

"Participating in the extreme sport is just an adrenaline rush, a sense or feeling that they can't get in any other setting."

Frey admits that isn't true for all extreme athletes. Those involved in the most dangerous sports such as B.A.S.E. jumping, he says, are on the fringe of the fringe. They don't always have absolute control over their fates and thus must realize they really are risking their very lives when they jump.

"I think the B.A.S.E. jumpers know," Frey says. "That's why the sky-divers think they're nuts. The sky-divers won't participate in B.A.S.E. jumping because they know there are too many elements they can't control. These (B.A.S.E. jumpers) have obviously taken it over the edge.

"When somebody does a B.A.S.E. jump off a bridge or say off a building, there are too many factors that can come into play. If you're jumping from a building in the heart of Chicago, what if a gust of wind comes up? That wind will throw them against another building and they'll be dead. That kind of sport is certainly death-defying because the risks are so much higher."

Still, extreme sports seem to be appealing to the masses more than ever. Frey believes today's mass media is at least partially to blame for that.

"There's a lot of television attention on it," he says. "These sports have all been transformed into major business enterprises. There's a lot of commercial return that comes from participating in some of theses sports. The television coverage results in sponsorships and equipment. You get publicity. If you're in a major commercial, you can make a lot of money."

Another factor in the increased popularity could be the X Generation isn't buying into the old standards in sports.

"There was a study that was recently released that suggests the 18-30-year-old crowd may be somewhat disenchanted with pro sports as we know them today – baseball, football, basketball," Frey says. "It may be interesting to see if this will have a generational affect on television and radio, if it affects advertising dollars or if it affects the willingness to go out and buy a ticket to a game.

"If it does, these guys may be more apt to go snowboarding than they are to go buy a ticket to the Mariners or the Bulls or the Cowboys."

And science is doing its part, engineering bodies that are bigger, stronger, faster and more durable. A generation ago, there were few people who could hang by their fingers for hours at a time as ice-climbers and rock-climbers now do. New methods of weight-training and dietary supplements are constructing humans with extraordinary abilities.

"We have something we call `mortal engines' where scientifically we are trying to find ways to take the human body beyond its physical limits," Frey says. "That's commonplace now and the extreme sports like sky-diving and rock-climbing and snowboarding all help you to meet new challenges.

"It's like the marathoners. The limits are always being pushed. They run times now they never dreamed of decades ago. They're assisted by the mechanization of training, the new machines that can build you beyond anything they had before."

But why extreme sports? Why now? Why does society seem more and more hell-bent toward these crazy pursuits? Frey believes it is a gathering trend.

"Society is changing," he says. "Everything is visceral now rather than cerebral. We have kids today who believe that if it feels good, you do it.

"We have gone from deferred gratification to immediate gratification, from long-term goals to short-term goals. That's what the X Generation is wanting and one of the reasons extreme sports are so appealing to them."

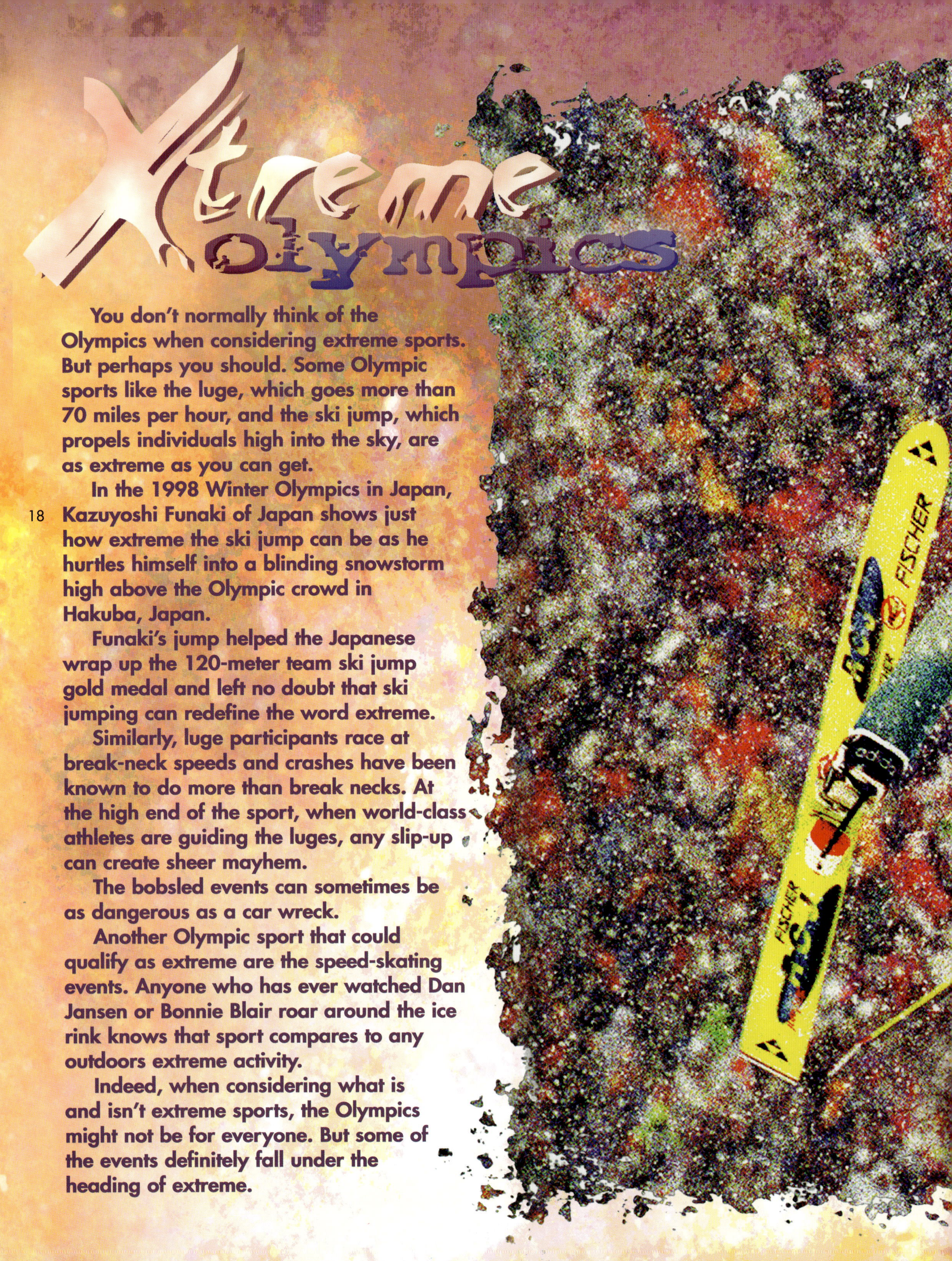

Xtreme Olympics

You don't normally think of the Olympics when considering extreme sports. But perhaps you should. Some Olympic sports like the luge, which goes more than 70 miles per hour, and the ski jump, which propels individuals high into the sky, are as extreme as you can get.

In the 1998 Winter Olympics in Japan, Kazuyoshi Funaki of Japan shows just how extreme the ski jump can be as he hurtles himself into a blinding snowstorm high above the Olympic crowd in Hakuba, Japan.

Funaki's jump helped the Japanese wrap up the 120-meter team ski jump gold medal and left no doubt that ski jumping can redefine the word extreme.

Similarly, luge participants race at break-neck speeds and crashes have been known to do more than break necks. At the high end of the sport, when world-class athletes are guiding the luges, any slip-up can create sheer mayhem.

The bobsled events can sometimes be as dangerous as a car wreck.

Another Olympic sport that could qualify as extreme are the speed-skating events. Anyone who has ever watched Dan Jansen or Bonnie Blair roar around the ice rink knows that sport compares to any outdoors extreme activity.

Indeed, when considering what is and isn't extreme sports, the Olympics might not be for everyone. But some of the events definitely fall under the heading of extreme.

1998
13
FISCHER
FISCHER

Xtreme definitions

There's more than one way to look at extreme sports. Offered here are Webster's staid definitions followed by some closer to reality versions of our own.

Sky diving

Webster's: (ski' • div ing), *n.* the sport of jumping from an airplane at a moderate or high altitude and free-falling and using one's body to control direction or movements before opening one's parachute.

McMillen's: Making the conscious decision to step out of an airplane into nothing but air, then gyrating wildly as you plummet several thousand feet before deploying a device you hope will open and help cushion your fall.

Hang gliding

Webster's: (hang' • glid ing), *n.* the sport of launching oneself from a cliff or steep incline and soaring through the air by means of a hang glider.

McMillen's: purposefully running and jumping off of a cliff or steep incline while clinging to a large, triangular, umbrella-like device and hoping it doesn't close.

Bodyboarding

Webster's: (bod' e bor' ding) *n.* the sport of riding ocean waves while holding onto a short, oblong or square board approximately half the length of a normal surfboard.

McMillen's: playing the Big Kahuna with a sawed-off surfboard that can be of little or no help when the wave gets too big or fast.

Street luge

Webster's: (stret' • loozh), *n.* a sport in which one- or two-person sleds equipped with roller wheels are used to race down steep inclines, usually on a course marked on streets at speeds often exceeding 70 mph.

McMillen's: lying prone on a gurney-like device while going 70-plus mph en route to another gurney-like device.

XTREME
Snowboarding

XTREME
B M X

XTREME
Ice-climbing

XTREME
B.A.S.E. jumping

XTREME
Wakeboarding

XTREME
Snowboarding

XTREME
Motocross

XTREME
Skateboarding

XTREME
Snowboarding

XTREME
Sky surfing

XTREME
Wakeboarding

Xtreme profile

BRENDA OLDFIELD

BASE jumping

Brenda Oldfield knows what it's like to be numbered among the "normal" sky-diving community, the people who consider themselves sane and rational.

Many of those sky-divers look askance at the world of B.A.S.E jumping, a pursuit they consider on the fringe of psychosis. To them, B.A.S.E. jumpers are pyorrhea.

"I can remember a few years ago when we'd point at them and talk about them," Oldfield says. "We'd say, `See those people over there. They're weirdos. Stay away from them.'"

That was how Oldfield looked at them more than 10 years ago. She had been sky diving, making more than 700 jumps, for five years before that. But a friend finally talked her into trying one of those daredevil jumps from a high fixed object. Then she was hooked. She became one of the "weirdos."

Now she just laughs at sky-divers who put B.A.S.E. jumpers down.

"Some B.A.S.E. jumpers kind of relish

B.A.S.E. jumping

B.A.S.E. jumping

people thinking that way about them," she says. "Others don't care either way. They irritated me initially with that attitude, but anymore I just laugh."

The thinking among many outside the sport is that B.A.S.E. jumping borders on the suicidal. There are 450 accredited B.A.S.E. jumpers in the world and Oldfield is No. 303.

The fact 39 of those 450 have died in pursuit of their sport, she says, is not indicative of the intent. Oldfield says the perception of her and her cohorts wanting to die is the opposite of reality.

"A common misconception in all extreme sports is that we have some weird death wish," says Oldfield, who has made more than 250 B.A.S.E. jumps. "It's actually just the opposite of that. I read once that someone said if you have any suicidal tendencies, sky diving would cure you of that. And it's true of B.A.S.E. jumping too.

"When you B.A.S.E. jump, just waking up in the morning is a wonderful experience. You can't wait to get to your next jump. If anything, it's an extreme life wish.

"When I started sky diving, I started wearing a seat belt. You don't want to die driving to a jump. You don't want to die stupidly."

Oldfield paused a moment and chuckled at her own words. She's well aware that many people see B.A.S.E. jumping as the ultimate in stupidity. Even her own parents wonder about her.

"They think I'm absolutely insane," she laughs. "My Dad keeps wondering where I came from."

Oldfield has found a kindred spirit with which to jump. Her significant other is Dennis McGlynn, B.A.S.E. jumper No. 262. They are a rarity in the B.A.S.E. jumping world, a couple who have jumped off bridges and antennas together, leaped from Angel Falls, the world's highest waterfall (3,212 feet) in Venezuela together and generally go hand-in-hand off all kinds of surfaces.

It is a way of life and Oldfield can't imagine any other. "It would devastate me not to be able to jump," she says. "I couldn't imagine life without it. I couldn't imagine sitting on a couch living vicariously. I've got to go experience life, not observe it."

B.A.S.E jumping

XTREME
Snow skiing

XTREME
Sky diving

XTREME
Snowboarding

XTREME
Rock-climbing

XTREME
B.A.S.E. jumping

XTREME
White-water rafting

XTREME
Snow skiing

XTREME
Snowboarding

XTREME
Wing walking

XTREME
Hang gliding

XTREME
Surfing

Sims

XTREME
BMX-freestyle

Snowboarding

Webster's: (sno' bord ing) *n.* riding on a board made for gliding on snow, the board resembling a wide ski to which both feet are secured and which one rides in an upright position.

McMillen's: riding a big board sideways on snow down a steep mountain with nothing to hang onto except your hat, or hopefully, your crash helmet.

Xtreme definitions

Webster's dictionary has one way of looking at extreme sports and we have another that might be considered extreme in itself. See which one fits your particular tastes the best.

Ice-climbing

Webster's: (is' • clim ing), *n.* a sport in which a person climbs on giant sheets of ice as on the side of glaciers.

McMillen's: actually scaling a huge ice cube with ice picks in your hands and on your feet when you are sober and not just pretending to do it while you are looking at your drink and passing out drunk.

Snow Skiing

Webster's (sno' • ske ing) *n.* traveling over the snow on a pair of long, slender runners made of wood, plastic or metal.

McMillen's: riding two very small boards with the help of a pair of ski poles on snow down a steep mountain.

Kayaking

Webster's: (ki' ak ing) *n.* to go or travel on a small Eskimo canoe with a skin cover on a light framework, made watertight by flexible closure around the waist of the occupant and propelled with a double-bladed paddle.

McMillen's: getting sealed into a small covered canoe and fighting down a river with only one weird paddle that has two paddling ends thus enabling you to travel inverted and submerged much of the time.

XTREME
Surfing

XTREME
Surfing

XTREME
Snow skiing

XTREME
Snowboarding

XTREME
Bodyboarding

XTREME
B.A.S.E. jumping

XTREME
Street luge

XTREME
Ice-climbing

XTREME
Snow skiing

XTREME
Balloon jumping

Xtreme profile

CHRISTIAN FLETCHER

Waves crash, boards collide, rocks come into play now and then and you have to watch out for the occasional 18-wheeler that roars through. But hurt? Nah. Not Christian Fletcher.

This day, Fletcher, world-class surfer, is hobbling slightly on a swollen foot he received while on a wakeboarding sabbatical. But he scoffs at the idea his adventurous ways on the waves have ever seriously sidelined him.

"I've had a lot of stitches through the years," Fletcher says. "Mostly in my head. You know, you hit boards, you hit rocks, other surfers run over you ...

"But I've never been really seriously injured. I have this swollen foot and I hurt my knee a little a few years back. But that's about it."

Sounds like a pretty rough life. To Christian Fletcher, it's not even a blip on the screen of adventure. The average person would long remember a single trip to the hospital and the exact number of stitches received in that traumatic tumble. Fletcher has lost count.

"I'm *NOT* the average person," he says. "Nobody who knows me would say I'm

Surfers

FLETCHER Surfing

the average person."

Indeed, he's not from the average family either. His father, Herbie Fletcher, is a life-long surfer who was responsible for many surfing innovations in the 1960s. His brother, 23-year-old Nathan, also is a world-class surfer but is perhaps known more for his daredevil exploits in motocross, such as long-jumping through fiery hoops at the Los Angeles Coliseum a la Evil Knievel.

Fletcher's grandfather, Walter Hoffman was the 1958-59 world tandem surfing champion and still surfs at the age of 67. And his aunt, Joyce Hoffman, is a four-time world champion surfer. You could say it runs in the family.

As do the natural injuries for everyone in the family but him. Fletcher acknowledges that surfing can be dangerous to some. Just not to him.

"My dad broke his back twice surfing," Fletcher says. "My brother and my aunt and my grandfather have broken bones too. But not me. I'm not any more skilled than them. I'm just lucky."

He has taken that good fortune into many pursuits trying just about everything imaginable, from skateboarding to motocross.

Snowboarding, wakeboarding, bodyboarding, windsurfing, you name it. If it moves and it's perilous, he has done it.

"I like most whatever I'm doing at the moment," he says. "But surfing is special. For one thing, when you fall, you fall on water. That's better than rocks or the ground or something hard."

And less damaging. If he really is just lucky though, it is luck combined with plenty of skill. Fletcher was on a surfboard as far back as he can remember. His only precise memory of the early days is winning his first contest 22 years ago – at the age of 5. He had been surfing "for a while" by then.

There have been plenty of victories since, including the single highest surfing payout ever – more than $30,000 – in San Clemente a few years back. He also was chosen Surf Magazine's 1996-97 top surfer. But those aren't Fletcher's proudest accomplishments. He enjoys more talking about the innovations he has brought to surfing.

Like the aerial moves he has helped establish as part of the fabric of modern-day surfing. Fletcher says they started simply and naturally, flying out of the waves as a matter of course. He learned how to control them and return to the wave for the breath-taking moves known simply as aerials.

It's also virtually his religion. Fletcher says you can get a celestial feeling on a wave you can find nowhere else.

"On the best days, the feeling is just unbelievable," Fletcher says. "It's hard to explain. I guess you could say you kind of feel one with nature.

"It's a godly experience. I don't really go to church much. I do go surfing."

And he intends on attending those services for as long as the seas crash.

"It's something I'll do forever," he says. "My grandpa's still surfing and I'm sure I will be at his age."

Surfing

XTREME
Bodyboarding

XTREME
Sky diving

XTREME
Wakeboarding

SCOTT

XTREME
B.A.S.E. jumping

XTREME
Surfing

XTREME
Rock-climbing

XTREME
Sky surfing

XTREME
Snow skiing

XTREME
Snowboarding

108

XTREME
Sky diving

Xtreme definitions

There are two sides to any definition, particularly when it comes to extreme sports. Here we present some more of Webster's and McMillen's, giving you two completely different perspectives.

Rock-climbing

Webster's: (rok′ • kli ming) *n.* scaling almost vertical rock faces with the help of certain mountain-climbing gear such as ropes, picks and gloves often to a considerable degree of altitude.

McMillen's: climbing when the mountain is just a colossal, sheer rock and if you fall, you generally fall on another colossal rock.

Mountain biking

Webster's: (moun′ tn • bi king) *n.* riding bicycles especially equipped for rugged, grueling terrain up and down very steep mountain inclines both on and off mountain trails.

McMillen's: going uphill on a bike until your thighs explode, then going downhill on it until your head explodes.

Whitewater rafting

Webster's: (hwit′ wo ter • raf ting) *n.* moving over or through rapids in a large raft usually made of rubber.

McMillen's: riding a wild bull with only a paddle in your hands.

113

Wakeboarding

Webster's: (wak' bor ding) *n.* the sport of riding over water on a large oblong board, similar to those used in surfing, while holding onto a rope that extends behind a powerboat, usually going back and forth over the wake from the boat in an attempt to lift yourself for flips and other acrobatic tricks.

McMillen's: riding a surfboard and trying to catch the waves made behind a speeding boat while hanging onto a rope that is connected to that boat going at speeds reaching enough knots to leave your body in a knot if you let go.

XTREME
White-water rafting

XTREME
Bodyboarding

XTREME
Snow skiing

XTREME
Sky diving

119

XTREME
Rock-climbing

122

XTREME
Surfing

XTREME
Wakeboarding

XTREME
Snow skiing

liquid force
DUFFS
Nautiques

XTREME
Wakeboarding

XTREME
Snowboarding

XTREME
Balloon jumping

GREGG NECRASON

Wakeboarding

For as far back as he could remember, Gregg Necrason had been gliding on the water on two relatively thin pieces of wood.

His parents say they got him up on water skis first when he was only two years old. The Necrasons lived by a lake in Winter Park, Fla., and water skiing was their lives. They skied virtually every day, competing frequently in state and national tournaments.

Gregg was good, too. He won a roomful of trophies to prove it by the time he was 12. That's when it hit him.

"I just got burned out," he says. "I was doing a lot of tournaments and was getting up every day before school to work out. I just got tired of it so my dad said if I didn't enjoy it any more, I could quit.

"I didn't want to get on anything on the water again. I wanted to get as far away from it as I could. I wanted to play soccer or ride bicycles or anything. Just not ski. I quit water skiing completely when I was 12."

And for four years, he didn't get back on

Wakeboarding

NECRASON Wakeboarding

the water. That's when he started watching an old family friend, Scott Byerly, ride on a new contraption – a wakeboard. The style – standing sideways – and the challenge of not just riding behind but repeatedly negotiating the wake of the boat, was intriguing.

Byerly, of course, went on to become a wakeboarding legend, winner of the 1995 world championships and considered by many the best in the profession. At 16, Necrason began wakeboarding with him frequently and started learning all the tricks.

Now Necrason too is a world-class wakeboarder. He was junior men's world champion in 1996. At 21, his future is bright and he couldn't be forced back on a pair of skis.

"Never," Necrason says. "I haven't skied in years and I don't ever intend to again. Water skiing is boring. Who wants to just ride behind a boat when you can wakeboard and do flips and invent new tricks? In wakeboarding, you can express yourself more."

And Necrason is expressing himself a lot now. Water skiing was too tame, too methodical, too repetitive. Wakeboarding, using the forever changing wake of the boat to lift, turn and flip you, has a new twist every day so Necrason doesn't foresee any burnout.

The natural combination of water skiing, snowboarding, surfing and skateboarding, wakeboarding is a sport that often sneers at its ancestry. Necrason disdains even mentioning wakeboarding and water skiing in the same breath.

"They're not really very similar at all," he says. "You're on the water and you have a rope in your hand is all. Beyond that, you can do so much more on a wakeboard. You can do full flips and 360s and invent things."

Like his "KGB" move, Necrason's most recent invention. He describes it as a "blind-side mobius," which is to say he does a 360 with a flip away from the boat. Why KGB? It's what his friend, Ryan Siebring, another star wakeboarder, named it when he first saw the move.

There are countless more moves to invent as well. "I think that's the time you feel the best," Necrason says. "When you've invented a move that really rips and you pull it off. It's one of the greatest feelings you can have."

Wakeboarding

XTREME
Sky diving

XTREME
B M X

Xtreme president

Even presidents can go to extremes. In March of 1997, former President George Bush jumped out of an airplane from 12,500 feet up and parachuted safely to the ground at the age of 72. It was the second jump of his life, but the first by choice. In 1944, at the age of 20, Bush was the youngest fighter pilot in the Navy when he jumped out of a burning plane that was shot down by Japanese fighters over the Pacific Ocean.

XTREME
President

XTREME
Surfing

Nautiques

XTREME
Snow skiing

XTREME
Sky surfing

XTREME
Snowboarding

XTREME
Ice-climbing

XTREME
Wing walking

Xtreme photographer

Tom Sanders

Tom Sanders is one of the world's most renowned aerial photographers. His work has appeared in such movies as *Tomorrow Never Dies*, *Terminal Velocity*, *Point Break* and *Goldeneye* and in dozens of magazines including *Life*, *Sports Illustrated*, *Time* and *People*. He is a major contributor to this book as well.

Sanders, 44, lives his profession. He is an accomplished sky-diver who jumps with his photographic subjects. He has more than 6,000 jumps in his 20-year career, including one as the official photographer of the George Bush sky-dive. Sanders is rated an expert by the United States Hang-Gliding Association and the U.S. Parachute Association.

"I love my job because I get to participate, not just film," Sanders says. "It's much more fun to be a cameraman who's participating. I not only watch people have fun, but I have the same fun with them."

Sanders is perhaps best known in Hollywood for his breath-taking work on the James Bond movie *The Living Daylights* in which the stars were filmed on a giant net trailing behind a C-130 aircraft.

His most harrowing experience came during the shooting of the movie *Drop Zone* in a night scene in which three assistants provided lighting on the actors. As planned,

Photographer

Sanders was the last to deploy his parachute — and it didn't open.

"I had to go to my auxiliary chute," he says. "That's not that unusual. That happens about once every thousand jumps or so. But the combination of that, shooting at night and having a very heavy camera on my head, made it probably my closest call. We were over water just outside of Miami and I landed in the street near the harbor."

Sanders' wife, Jan Davis, also is an expert sky-diver who is the first woman to jump off Angel Falls in Venezuela. She is a professional sky-diver, wing-walker and B.A.S.E. jumper. Together they operate their photography business, Aerial Focus, out of Santa Barbara, Calif.,

B.A.S.E. jumping

Webster's: (bas' • jum ping) *n.* a specialized and often illegal form of parachuting from four kinds of fixed structures which include buildings, large radio antennas, spans or bridges and earth or cliffs.

McMillen's: trying to figure out four different ways of committing suicide without admitting you're doing it even once.

Xtreme definitions

With extreme sports, Webster's dictionary can only take you so far. So to expand the definition and the perception, we've added the McMillen way of looking at extreme sports.

Skateboarding

Webster's: (skat' bor ding) *n.* the sport of riding upon, usually while standing, a device that consists of a short, oblong piece of wood, plastic or aluminum mounted on large roller-skate wheels; riding on smooth surfaces and requiring better balance of the rider than ordinary roller skates do.

McMillen's: riding on too short a board down too long a sidewalk or too steep a road for too long a time.

Wing-walking

Webster's: (wing' • wal king) *n.* the sport of climbing out on the wing of a moving airplane, usually a smaller propeller-type biplane, while attached to the surface by a rope or wire.

McMillen's: playing the Great Waldo Pepper while hoping no birds are in the very near vicinity.

In-line Skating

Webster's: (in' lin • ska ting) *n.* riding on skates on which the four wheels are directly in a line, usually while attempting to scale specially devised structures called half-pipes made of wood or concrete and other fixed edifices or frameworks.

McMillen's: ice-skating on rollers without ice on surfaces harder than ice and more likely to bloody your nose or other parts of the anatomy.

Angel Falls

Angel Falls in Venezuela is the world's highest waterfall at 3,212 feet and is a favorite destination for B.A.S.E. jumpers around the world. The falls offer not only a spectacular view, but a magnificent base from which to jump and a beautiful valley in which to land. One such B.A.S.E. jumper takes in all that breath-taking panorama on Page 164.

XTREME
B.A.S.E. jumping

XTREME
Kayaking

XTREME
Ice-climbing

XTREME
Motocross

XTREME
B.A.S.E. jumping

XTREME
Wakeboarding

XTREME
Wakeboarding

XTREME
Snow skiing

XTREME
Surfing

XTREME
Snowboarding

Xtreme profile

STEVE GRAHAM

Snowboarding

Steve Graham feels old.

In the ever-changing world of snowboarding, perhaps he is a little old at 30. But he certainly hasn't slowed down any.

It's just that as he watches the new stars evolving in the sport of snowboarding, Graham is one of the few who can think back a decade or more and remember what it used to be like. He recalls how the first snowboards were little more than whittled-down versions of old surf boards.

"What's really neat is to think about the equipment we have now," Graham says. "It's so much more advanced. The guys coming up today don't have to put in the years we did with the crappy boards and other poor equipment we were forced to use."

If anyone knows about those things, it is Graham, one of the real pioneers of snowboarding. Graham first saw a snowboard in Europe in 1985, years before most Americans had ever heard of them. He watched video of another pioneer, Regis Rolland, then and was immediately hooked.

Graham had skied his entire life, starting out at the tender age of four. But this snowboarding, he thought, was something completely different.

"The first time I saw it was on one of Regis' videos on a television in a bar in Leysin,

Snowboarding

GRAHAM Snowboarding

Switzerland," Graham says. "My dad was working overseas and I had a chance to ski at some great places.

"But snowboarding looked really cool. The first time I tried it, I fell in love with it. I didn't care for the hard plastic boots you have to use with skis. I've lost too many toenails in those boots, so I was pretty tired of skiing.

"Since I first picked up a snowboard, I haven't skied again. And I never will. Skiing just doesn't compare. There's just a lack of freedom with ski boots that you don't have on a snowboard. You are really so heavy on the snow on skis. But you can just jump on a board and go.

"And you're actually safer on a snowboard. You're not as likely to twist a knee on a snowboard."

Not that Graham has ever chosen the safe way to live. He has been on surfboards, skateboards, motorcycles and skis most of his life. He is considered one of snowboard's greatest innovators and is a virtual legend in the sport.

And being 30 doesn't mean the game has slowed him down. He still snowboards all over the world and can be found at the big air tournaments in Europe where prize money often reaches $100,000.

Graham's greatest celebrity probably has come from his many snowboarding videos, starting with the popular "Snowboarders in Exile" and "Western Front" and the classic "Riders on the Storm." He has appeared on television and in magazines around the world. Smirnoff vodka even named a drink after him, the "Steve Graham."

"Yeah, I've been around a while and a lot of the friends I started out with are no longer in snowboarding," Graham admits. "But I've been lucky enough to adapt to the different riding styles and keep up with the guys coming up. I still love to ride."

He can't say for certain how much longer he'll snowboard. He has his own snowboard company now and the endorsements from such companies as Quiksilver are still good. But he knows someday it will end.

"It's still fun for me so who knows?" he says. "I guess when I get too old and lazy, I'll hang them up. But for now, I still feel young enough to get up there with the best of them."

Snowboarding

XTREME
Surfing

XTREME
Snow skiing

XTREME
Wakeboarding

XTREME
Bodyboarding

XTREME
Surfing

XTREME
Snowboarding

XTREME
Wakeboarding

XTREME
B.A.S.E. jumping

XTREME
Surfing

XTREME
Balloon jumping

XTREME
Wakeboarding

XTREME
Snowboarding

SIMS

SECTOR

XTREME
Sky surfing

Xtreme definitions

Surfing

Webster's: (surf' ing) *n.* a sport in which a person stands or lies prone on a surfboard and rides the crest of a breaking wave toward the shore.

McMillen's: standing on a very large, slick board that is propelled by an even larger wave while trying very hard not to fall off.

Webster's dictionary gives you only the bare-bones definition, simple and to the point. For a more visceral look at extreme sports, we offer the McMillen's dictionary of terms.

Sky Surfing

Webster's: (ski' • sur fing) *n.* the sport of parachuting out of airplanes while having a long, oblong board attached to your feet and doing aerial acrobatics before deploying the parachute.

McMillen's: forgetting where you are when you go surfing then realizing it and hoping someone remembered to strap a parachute to your back.

Balloon jumping

Webster's: (ba' loon • jum' ping) *n.* the sport of parachuting out of hot-air balloons.

McMillen's: going on a hot-air balloon ride, then after reaching the highest point, losing your mind and deciding to jump out.

Motocross

Webster's: (mo' to cros) *n.* a motorcycle race over a closed course consisting of a winding dirt trail with hills, jumps, sharp turns and often muddy terrain.

McMillen's: Marlon Brando in *The Wild One* having a very bad day.

XTREME
Bodyboarding

XTREME
In-line skating

XTREME
Snow skiing

214

XTREME
Ice-climbing

HONDA
HONDA
19

XTREME
Wakeboarding

XTREME
Sky diving

XTREME
Snowboarding

XTREME
Ice-climbing

Xtreme profile

MIKE STEWART

Bodyboarding

Like many world renowned bodyboarders and surfers, Mike Stewart has been in his share of

movies. They were mostly of the pure action variety, lots of scenes of bodyboarding and surfing.

But this was something different.

This time, Stewart met up with Zalman King, the avant-garde director of Hollywood's provocative "9 1/2 Weeks" and other eccentric films. And this time Stewart was being asked not only to ride the surf, but act.

"I've been in a bunch of surfer movies," Stewart says. "But this was the first time I've had a speaking role. It was real interesting."

That's putting it diplomatically. Actually, this acting stuff was not Stewart's cup of tea, though his role as one of three surfers in King's movie "In God's Hands," has been well received.

"It's just a movie about the lives of these guys," he says. "It's kind of looking at life through their eyes. It tries to evoke some of the feelings of being a surfer.

Bodyboarding

STEWART Bodyboarding

"If you're looking for a deep story-line, you won't find it here. It's more of an esoteric blend of the life of a surfer."

Stewart did his best but doesn't claim to be the next Robert Redford.

"I guess it was pretty cool to do once," Stewart says. "But basically, I'm opposed to acting. I'd rather be actually doing something than acting like I'm doing it.

"I devised a term for what I do. I call it `hacting.' I pretty much hack at acting more than anything else."

It is one of very few pursuits that Stewart has not taken to particularly well. His life is as eclectic as it is hectic. Stewart has been involved in a surfing book called "Jaws," has his own fin company and even dabbles in product design.

He's most noted, of course, for his bodyboarding exploits – nine times world champion in that sport – and also is unbeaten in body surfing. Bodyboarding has been his signature sport for some 25 years, since he was a small boy growing up in Hawaii.

"Living in Hawaii, it was kind of natural to get into surfing," says Stewart. "In Hawaii, there are different kinds of surf. There are the kind that break softly and the kind that break hollow, the more powerful waves.

"Those waves are the kind that I was exposed to the most. So I took up bodyboarding to handle the hollow waves better. The difference is that with bodyboarding, you have a lower center of gravity. The boards are kinetic in nature in that they bend and flex more. So you're able to control the speed more."

At 34, Stewart doesn't feel he has slowed down appreciably.

"In some respects maybe I have," he says. "But for the most part, everything I do is more sped up and I am more efficient at doing it because of my experience. So I'm able to do more different things than I did when I was younger.

"I'm not planning retirement. I still have some challenges in the sport and I still am exploring ideas in product design."

Just not any more dramatic acting. He'd rather do than act.

Bodyboarding

XTREME
Wing walking

XTREME
Wakeboarding

XTREME
Snow skiing

XTREME
Surfing

Palmer

XTREME
Snowboarding

XTREME
Rock-climbing

XTREME
Motocross

XTREME
Skateboarding

XTREME
Surfing

XTREME
Snowboarding

BLINK 182
THE WAVE
PIT LINE
REEF

XTREME
Kayaking

XTREME
Hang gliding

Xtreme equipment

In many cases, extreme sports require extreme equipment. That equipment is often vital for improved maneuverability and handling, but even more so for protection, as in the case of high-impact crash helmets for such sports as sky-diving and B.A.S.E. jumping. On these pages are some examples of various gear available for several sports from surfing to wakeboarding to sky-diving.

Included are some of the top-of-the-line snowboards, the best parachutes in the business and first-quality bindings for snowboards. Also pictured on these pages are surfboard pads for better traction and special bindings for wakeboards.

These kinds of equipment are for the serious extreme athlete. This and many other accessories can be purchased at the equipment companies listed below as well as at sporting goods stores everywhere.

PALMER – Snowboards
PALMER – Snowboard Bindings
BADASS Bindings – Wakeboard Bindings

SQUAREONE – Parachute Containers SQUAREONE – Sky Diving Helmets ASTRO DECK – Surfboard Traction Pads

XTREME
Kayaking

254

Installing the XTREME SPORTS screen saver.

1. This program requires that you be running Windows 95, Windows 98 or Windows NT workstation. The program files require approximately 2MB of free space on your hard drive.

2. If you are using Windows 95 or Windows 98, the installation program should start when you insert the CD-ROM disk into your drive.

3. If it does not automatically start, or if you are using Windows NT, open up the "My Computer" folder, double-click on the icon that represents your CD-ROM drive and double-click on the program icon "SETUP.EXE".

4. The program will prompt you to choose a location for the files. When installation is complete it will set this screen saver to be your active one.

5. If this screen saver is not set as your active one, you can set it to be by clicking on the "START" button and selecting SETTINGS>CONTROL PANEL>DISPLAY and then the "SCREEN SAVER" tab. From the screen saver list choose "XTREME SPORTS" and click on "APPLY".